THE 30-MINUTE SHAKESPEARE
ROMEO AND JULIET

"Nick Newlin's work as a teaching artist for Folger Education during the past thirteen years has provided students, regardless of their experience with Shakespeare or being on stage, a unique opportunity to tread the boards at the Folger Theatre. Working with students to edit Shakespeare's plays for performance at the annual Folger Shakespeare Festivals has enabled students to gain new insights into the Bard's plays, build their skills of comprehension and critical reading, and just plain have fun working collaboratively with their peers.

Folger Education promotes performance-based teaching of Shakespeare's plays, providing students with an interactive approach to Shakespeare's plays in which they participate in a close reading of the text through intellectual, physical, and vocal engagement. Newlin's *The 30-Minute Shakespeare* series is an invaluable resource for teachers of Shakespeare, and for all who are interested in performing the plays."

ROBERT YOUNG, PH.D.
DIRECTOR OF EDUCATION
FOLGER SHAKESPEARE LIBRARY

Romeo and Juliet: The 30-Minute Shakespeare
ISBN 978-1-935550-01-3
Adaptation, essays, and notes © 2010 by Nick Newlin

Cover design by Sarah Juckniess
Printed in the United States of America

Distributed by Consortium Book Sales & Distribution
www.cbsd.com

NICOLO WHIMSEY PRESS
www.nicolowhimsey.com

Art Director: Sarah Juckniess
Managing Editor: Katherine Little

THE MOST EXCELLENT
and LAMENTABLE TRAGEDIE

of

ROMEO AND JULIET

THE 30-MINUTE SHAKESPEARE

Written by WILLIAM SHAKESPEARE

Abridged AND Edited
by NICK NEWLIN

Nicolo Whimsey
Press

Brandywine, MD

To my Mom,
Louisa Newlin
Thanks for the
inspiration and support.

Special thanks to Joanne Flynn, Bill Newlin, Eliza Newlin Carney, William and Louisa Newlin, Michael Tolaydo, Hilary Kacser, Sarah Juckniess, Katherine Little, Eva Zimmerman, Julie Schaper and all of Consortium, Leo Bowman and the students, faculty, and staff at Banneker Academic High School, and Robert Young PhD, and the Folger Shakespeare Library, especially the wonderful Education Department.

✳ TABLE OF CONTENTS

✳ NO EXPERIENCE NECESSARY

I was not a big "actor type" in high school, so if you weren't either, or if the young people you work with are not, then this book is for you. Whether or not you work with "actor types," you can use this book to stage a lively and captivating thirty-minute version of a Shakespeare play. No experience is necessary.

When I was about eleven years old, my parents took me to see Shakespeare's *Two Gentlemen of Verona,* which was being performed as a Broadway musical. I didn't comprehend every word I heard, but I was enthralled with the language, the characters, and the story, and I understood enough of it to follow along. From then on, I associated Shakespeare with *fun.*

Of course Shakespeare is fun. The Elizabethan audiences knew it, which is one reason he was so popular. It didn't matter that some of the language eluded them. The characters were passionate and vibrant, and their conflicts were compelling. Young people study Shakespeare in high school, but more often than not they read his work like a text book and then get quizzed on academic elements of the play, such as plot, theme, and vocabulary. These are all very interesting, but not nearly as interesting as standing up and performing a scene! It is through performance that the play comes alive and all its "academic" elements are revealed. There is nothing more satisfying to a student or teacher than the feeling of "owning" a Shakespeare play, and that can only come from performing it.

But Shakespeare's plays are often two or more hours long, making the performance of an entire play almost out of the question. One can perform a single scene, which is certainly a good start, but what about the story? What about the changes a character goes through as the play progresses? When school groups perform one scene unedited, or when they lump several plays together, the audience can get lost. This is why I have always preferred to tell the story of the play.

The 30-Minute Shakespeare gives students and teachers a chance to get up on their feet and act out a Shakespeare play in half an hour, using his language. The emphasis is on key scenes, with narrative bridges between scenes to keep the audience caught up on the action. The stage directions are built into this script so that young actors do not have to stand in one place; they can move and tell the story with their actions as well as their words. And it can all be done in a classroom during class time!

That is where this book was born: not in a research library, a graduate school lecture, a professional stage, or even an after-school drama club. All of the play cuttings in *The 30-Minute Shakespeare* were first rehearsed in a D.C. public high school English class, and performed successfully at the Folger Shakespeare Library's annual Secondary School Shakespeare Festival. The players were not necessarily "actor types." For many of them, this was their first performance in a play.

Something almost miraculous happens when students perform Shakespeare. They "get" it. By occupying the characters and speaking the words out loud, students gain a level of understanding and appreciation that is unachievable by simply reading the text. That is the magic of a performance-based method of learning Shakespeare, and this book makes the formerly daunting task of staging a Shakespeare play possible for anybody.

With *The 30-Minute Shakespeare* book series I hope to help teachers and students produce a Shakespeare play in a short amount of time, thus jump-starting the process of discovering the beauty, magic, and fun of the Bard. Plot, theme, and language reveal themselves through the performance of these half-hour play cuttings, and everybody involved receives the priceless gift of "owning" a piece of Shakespeare. The result is an experience that is fun and engaging, and one that we can all carry with us as we play out our own lives on the stages of the world.

NICK NEWLIN
Brandywine, MD
March 2010

CHARACTERS IN THE PLAY

The following is a list of characters that appear in this cutting. For the full breakdown of characters, see Sample Program.

ROMEO: Montague's son

JULIET: Capulet's daughter

MERCUTIO: Kinsman to the Prince and friend to Romeo

TYBALT: Lady Capulet's nephew and Juliet's cousin

THE NURSE: Juliet's nursemaid

FRIAR LAURENCE: A brother of the Franciscan order

CAPULET: Juliet's father, feuding with Montagues

LADY CAPULET: Capulet's wife, Juliet's mother

PARIS: A noble young kinsman to the Prince

BENVOLIO: Montague's nephew, and friend to Romeo

MONTAGUE: Romeo's father, feuding with Capulets

LADY MONTAGUE: Montague's wife, Romeo's mother

BALTHASAR: Romeo's servant

PRINCE: Prince Escalus, Prince of Verona

SAMPSON: A servant of the Capulet household

GREGORY: A servant of the Capulet household

PROLOGUE SPEAKER

CITIZENS (includes brawling Montagues and Capulets)

NARRATORS

SOUND OPERATOR *plays* Sound Cue #1 ("Intro"), *fading out when* **SPEAKER** *stops walking.*

✳ PROLOGUE

SPEAKER *enters from stage rear curtain and walks downstage center.*

> Two households, both alike in dignity,
> In fair Verona, where we lay our scene,
> From ancient grudge break to new mutiny,
> Where civil blood makes civil hands unclean.
> From forth the fatal loins of these two foes
> A pair of star-cross'd lovers take their life;
> Whose misadventured piteous overthrows
> Do with their death bury their parents' strife.
> The fearful passage of their death-mark'd love,
> And the continuance of their parents' rage,
> Which, but their children's end, nought could remove,
> Is now the two hours' traffic of our stage;
> The which if you with patient ears attend,
> What here shall miss, our toil shall strive to mend.

Exit **SPEAKER** *stage left.*

✳ **SCENE 1.** (ACT I, SCENE I)

Verona. A public place.

Enter SAMPSON *and* GREGORY, *armed with swords, from back of audience. They come to stage left.*

SAMPSON
> I will take the wall of any man or maid of Montague's.

GREGORY
> The quarrel is between our masters and us their men.

SAMPSON
> When I have fought with the men, I will be cruel
> with the maids, and cut off their heads.

GREGORY
> The heads of the maids?

SAMPSON
> Ay, the heads of the maids, or their maidenheads.

GREGORY *(looking stage left)*
> Draw thy tool! here comes
> two of the house of the Montagues.

SAMPSON
> I will bite my thumb at them;
> which is a disgrace to them, if they bear it.

Enter ABRAHAM *and* BALTHASAR *from rear of audience. They come to stage right.*

SAMPSON *bites thumb.*

ABRAHAM
> Do you bite your thumb at us, sir?

SAMPSON
> I do bite my thumb, sir.

ABRAHAM *(wanting to draw sword but resisting)*
> Do you bite your thumb at us, sir?

SAMPSON
> *(Aside to* GREGORY*)*
> Is the law of our side, if I say ay?

GREGORY
> No.

SAMPSON
> No, sir, I do not bite my thumb at you, sir,
> but I bite my thumb, sir.

SAMPSON *bites thumb again, somewhat directed at audience.*

GREGORY
> Do you quarrel, sir?

ABRAHAM
> Quarrel sir! no, sir.

SAMPSON
> Draw, if you be men. Gregory, remember thy
> washing blow.

SAMPSON *pushes* GREGORY *toward* ABRAHAM *and* BALTHASAR.

Enter BENVOLIO *from rear of audience.*

BENVOLIO
>Part, fools!
>Put up your swords; you know not what you do.
>*(beats down their swords)*

Enter TYBALT *from stage left, coming in quickly.*

TYBALT *(standing between* SAMPSON *and* GREGORY*)*
>*to* BENVOLIO
>What, art thou drawn among these heartless hinds?
>Turn thee, Benvolio, look upon thy death.

BENVOLIO
>I do but keep the peace: put up thy sword,
>Or manage it to part these men with me.

TYBALT
>What, drawn, and talk of peace! I hate the word,
>As I hate hell, all Montagues, and thee:
>Have at thee, coward!

TYBALT *draws sword,* BENVOLIO *blocks, pushes* TYBALT,
TYBALT *swings,* BENVOLIO *ducks under.*

SOUND OPERATOR *plays* Sound Cue #2 ("Fight Music").

As the music plays, the TWO CAPULET YOUTH *and the* TWO
MONTAGUE YOUTH *fight in slow motion.*

FIRST CITIZEN
>Clubs, bills, and partisans! strike! beat them down!
>Down with the Capulets! down with the Montagues!

Enter CAPULET, *in his gown, and* LADY CAPULET *from stage left, coming center stage, near stage left pillar.*

CAPULET

> What noise is this? Give me my long sword, ho!

LADY CAPULET

> Why call you for a sword?

CAPULET

> My sword, I say! Old Montague is come,
> And flourishes his blade in spite of me.

Enter MONTAGUE *and* LADY MONTAGUE *from stage right.*

MONTAGUE

> Thou villain Capulet!—Hold me not, let me go.

LADY MONTAGUE

> Thou shalt not stir a foot to seek a foe.

CAPULET YOUTHS *and* MONTAGUE YOUTHS *fight in super slow motion.* TYBALT *and* BENVOLIO *stand on either side of the crowd, wanting to fight but unable to because the crowd is in their way.*

Enter PRINCE *from audience rear.*

When PRINCE *steps on the stage,* SOUND OPERATOR *stops music. Beginning with* ONE CAPULET YOUTH, *each person notices* PRINCE *individually, stopping and backing/bowing away.*

PRINCE *(very loud and angrily)*

> Rebellious subjects, enemies to peace,
> What, ho! you men, you beasts,
> On pain of torture, from those bloody hands
> Throw your mistemper'd weapons to the ground,

And hear the sentence of your moved prince.
Three civil brawls, bred of an airy word,
By thee, old Capulet, and Montague,
Have thrice disturb'd the quiet of our streets,
If ever you disturb our streets again,
Your lives shall pay the forfeit of the peace.
On pain of death, all men depart.

Exeunt all but MONTAGUE, LADY MONTAGUE, *and* BENVOLIO.

CAPULETS *exit stage left,* MONTAGUES *exit stage right.*

MONTAGUE

Who set this ancient quarrel new abroach?
Speak, nephew, were you by when it began?

BENVOLIO

The fiery Tybalt, with his sword prepared,
He swung about his head and cut the winds,
While we were interchanging thrusts and blows,
Till the prince came, who parted either part.

LADY MONTAGUE

O, where is Romeo? saw you him to-day?
Right glad I am he was not at this fray.

BENVOLIO

Madam, an hour before the worshipp'd sun
Peer'd forth the golden window of the east,
underneath the grove of sycamore
So early walking did I see your son.

MONTAGUE

Many a morning hath he there been seen,
With tears augmenting the fresh morning dew.
Adding to clouds more clouds with his deep sighs;

Could we but learn from whence his sorrows grow.
We would as willingly give cure as know.

Enter ROMEO *from stage rear.*

BENVOLIO

See, where he comes: so please you, step aside;
I'll know his grievance, or be much denied.

MONTAGUE

Come, madam, let's away.

Exeunt MONTAGUE *and* LADY MONTAGUE *stage right.*

BENVOLIO

Good-morrow, cousin.

ROMEO

Is the day so young?

BENVOLIO

But new struck nine.

ROMEO

Ay me! sad hours seem long.
    (leans against stage left pillar)

BENVOLIO

What sadness lengthens Romeo's hours?

ROMEO

Not having that, which, having, makes them short.

BENVOLIO

In love?

ROMEO

Out—

BENVOLIO

Of love?

ROMEO

Out of her favour, where I am in love.
(walks a few steps downstage center)
Love is a smoke raised with the fume of sighs;
Being purged, a fire sparkling in lovers' eyes;
What is it else? a madness most discreet,
In sadness, cousin, I do love a woman.

BENVOLIO

I aim'd so near, when I supposed you loved.

ROMEO

A right good mark-man! And she's fair I love.

BENVOLIO

A right fair mark, fair coz, is soonest hit.

ROMEO

O, she is rich in beauty, only poor,
That when she dies with beauty dies her store.

BENVOLIO

Then she hath sworn that she will still live chaste?

ROMEO

She hath, and in that sparing makes huge waste,
She hath forsworn to love, and in that vow
Do I live dead that live to tell it now.

BENVOLIO

> Be ruled by me, forget to think of her.

ROMEO

> O, teach me how I should forget to think.

BENVOLIO

> By giving liberty unto thine eyes;
> Examine other beauties.

ROMEO

> He that is strucken blind cannot forget
> The precious treasure of his eyesight lost:
> Farewell: thou canst not teach me to forget.

BENVOLIO

> I'll pay that doctrine, or else die in debt.

Exeunt stage right.

TWO STAGEHANDS *take bench and place it at an acute angle stage right to face stage left and audience*

✳ SCENE 2. (ACT II, SCENE II)

Capulet's orchard.

NARRATOR *enters from stage rear curtain and walks downstage center.*

> Romeo and a group of Montague friends crash a
> party at the Capulets. Romeo and Juliet, a Capulet,
> see each other for the first time, and fall in love,
> discovering afterward that they are from enemy
> families. Later that night, Romeo climbs a wall and
> enters Capulet's garden. Love is blind.

Enter JULIET *from stage right. She stands on bench, stage right,
as though it is a balcony. Enter* ROMEO *from stage rear, acting
as if he is climbing up the balcony wall (though he is really
climbing the floor!). He then stands beside stage right pillar.*

ROMEO
> He jests at scars that never felt a wound.
> > *(sees* JULIET *standing on bench)*
> But, soft! what light through yonder window breaks?
> It is the east, and Juliet *(pauses)* is the sun.
> Arise, fair sun, and kill the envious moon,
> Who is already sick and pale with grief,
> That thou her maid art far more fair than she:
> > *(turns toward audience; in a stage whisper)*
> It is my lady, O, it is my love!
> O, that she knew she were!

JULIET *(straight out toward audience)*
> O Romeo, Romeo! wherefore art thou Romeo?
> Deny thy father and refuse thy name;
> Or, if thou wilt not, be but sworn my love,
> And I'll no longer be a Capulet.

ROMEO *(aside)*
> Shall I hear more, or shall I speak at this?

*(**ROMEO** sneaks around bench behind **JULIET**)*

JULIET
> 'Tis but thy name that is my enemy;
> Thou art thyself, though not a Montague.
> What's Montague? it is nor hand, nor foot,
> Nor arm, nor face, nor any other part
> Belonging to a man. O, be some other name!
> What's in a name? that which we call a rose
> By any other name would smell as sweet;
> So Romeo would, were he not Romeo call'd,
> Retain that dear perfection which he owes
> Without that title. Romeo, doff thy name,
> And for that name which is no part of thee
> Take all myself.

ROMEO *(who is now standing right behind **JULIET** on bench)*
> I take thee at thy word:
> > *(**JULIET** screams, almost falls; **ROMEO** catches her)*
> Call me but love, and I'll be new baptized;
> Henceforth I never will be Romeo.

JULIET *(still very agitated)*
> How camest thou hither, tell me, and wherefore?
> The orchard walls are high and hard to climb,
> > *(gestures stage rear)*
> And the place death, considering who thou art,

If any of my kinsmen find thee here.
If they do see thee, they will murder thee.

ROMEO

Alack, there lies more peril in thine eye
Than twenty of their swords:

JULIET

I would not for the world they saw thee here.

ROMEO

My life were better ended by their hate,
Than death prorogued, *(pause)* wanting of thy love.

JULIET

Thou know'st the mask of night is on my face,
Else would a maiden blush bepaint my cheek
For that which thou hast heard me speak to-night
O gentle Romeo,
If thou dost love, pronounce it faithfully:
Or if thou think'st I am too quickly won,
I'll frown and be perverse an say thee nay,
    (turns away)

ROMEO

Lady, by yonder blessed moon I swear
That tips with silver all these fruit-tree tops—

JULIET *(turns back)*

O, swear not by the moon, the inconstant moon,
That monthly changes in her circled orb,
Lest that thy love prove likewise variable.

ROMEO

What shall I swear by?

JULIET

Well, do not swear: although I joy in thee,
I have no joy of this contract to-night:
It is too rash, too unadvised, too sudden;
This bud of love, by summer's ripening breath,
May prove a beauteous flower when next we meet.

ROMEO

O, wilt thou leave me so unsatisfied?

JULIET

What satisfaction canst thou have to-night?

ROMEO

The exchange of thy love's faithful vow for mine.

NURSE *(calls from within)*
Lady! Lady Juliet!

JULIET

I hear some noise within; dear love, adieu!
Anon, good nurse!
Three words, dear Romeo, and good night indeed.
(holds ROMEO'S *hands in front of her)*
If that thy bent of love be honourable,
Thy purpose marriage, send me word to-morrow,
And all my fortunes at thy foot I'll lay
And follow thee my lord throughout the world.

*(*JULIET *takes off a ring and holds it out to* ROMEO, *who happily pockets this token of her love.)*

ROMEO

So thrive my soul—

ROMEO *"climbs" off the bench and starts to "climb" backward upstage toward rear curtain. He stands up again after reaching the curtain.*

JULIET

> A thousand times good night!
> > *(starts to exit stage rear)*
> Good night,
> > *(pauses, comes back to hold* ROMEO'S *hands again)*
> good night!
> > *(pauses)*
> parting is such sweet sorrow,
> That I shall say good night till it be morrow.

Exit JULIET *stage right, pausing, and giving* ROMEO *one last glance or wave before exiting.*

ROMEO

> Sleep dwell upon thine eyes, peace in thy breast!
> Would I were sleep and peace, so sweet to rest.

Exit ROMEO *stage rear.*

STAGEHANDS ONE AND TWO *move bench to center stage for next scene.*

✳ **SCENE 3.** (ACT III, SCENE V)

Capulet's home.

NARRATOR *enters from stage rear.*

ROMEO *and* **JULIET** *enter simultaneously from stage left and take their positions;* **ROMEO** *sits on right, in front of bench, and* **JULIET** *lies on bench, sleeping.*

> Romeo and Juliet are secretly married by Friar
> Lawrence, but their joy does not last long. As
> Romeo tries to break up a fight, Juliet's cousin Tybalt
> kills Romeo's friend Mercutio. In revenge, Romeo
> kills Tybalt, and the Prince banishes Romeo from
> Verona. Romeo and Juliet spend their wedding night
> together, but must leave each other at dawn.

NARRATOR *exit stage left.*

JULIET *(awakens and sees Romeo)*
> Wilt thou be gone? it is not yet near day:
> It was the nightingale, and not the lark,
> That pierced the fearful hollow of thine ear;

ROMEO
> It was the lark, the herald of the morn,
> I must be gone and live, or stay and die.

JULIET

> Hie hence, be gone, away!
> It is the lark that sings so out of tune,
> More light and light it grows.

ROMEO

> More light and light; more dark and dark our woes!

Enter NURSE *from stage rear.*

NURSE *(in a panic)*
> Madam!

JULIET

> Nurse?

NURSE

> Your lady mother is coming to your chamber:
> The day is broke; be wary, look about.

Exit NURSE *stage rear.*

JULIET

> Then, window, let day in, and let life out.
> > *(opens window while facing audience)*

ROMEO

> Farewell, farewell! one kiss, and I'll descend.
> > *(they kiss)*

ROMEO *crosses down stage right.*

JULIET *(frightened, upset)*
> O God, I have an ill-divining soul!
> Methinks I see thee, now thou art below,

As one dead in the bottom of a tomb:
Either my eyesight fails, or thou look'st pale.

ROMEO (*responding, but still "cheating out"*)
And trust me, love, in my eye so do you:
Dry sorrow drinks our blood. Adieu, adieu!

Exit ROMEO *stage right.*

JULIET (*straight out to audience*)
O fortune, fortune! all men call thee fickle:
Be fickle, fortune;
For then, I hope, thou wilt not keep him long,
But send him back.

LADY CAPULET (*from within, stage rear*)
Ho, daughter! are you up?

JULIET
Who is't that calls? is it my lady mother?

Enter LADY CAPULET *from stage rear.*

LADY CAPULET
Why, how now, Juliet!

JULIET (*turns away from her, stage right*)
Madam, I am not well.

LADY CAPULET (*comforts* JULIET, *tentatively putting a hand on her shoulder*)
Evermore weeping for your cousin's death?
What, wilt thou wash him from his grave with tears?
But now I'll tell thee joyful tidings, girl.
(JULIET *turns, interested*)
Early next Thursday morn,

> The gallant, young and noble gentleman,
> The County Paris, at Saint Peter's Church,
> Shall happily make thee there a joyful bride.

JULIET (*tears herself away, backing up stage right*)
> He shall not make me there a joyful bride.
> I will not marry yet; and, when I do, I swear,
> It shall be Romeo, whom you know I hate,
> Rather than Paris.

LADY CAPULET
> Here comes your father; tell him so yourself,

LADY CAPULET *moves stage left.*

Enter CAPULET *and* NURSE *from stage rear.*

NURSE *stands stage right behind* JULIET, LADY CAPULET *stage left.* JULIET *and* CAPULET *stand center, with* JULIET *to stage right of* CAPULET.

CAPULET
> How now! a conduit, girl? what, still in tears?
> How now, wife!
> Have you deliver'd to her our decree?

LADY CAPULET
> Ay, sir; but she will none, she gives you thanks.
> I would the fool were married to her grave!

CAPULET (*astounded, center stage*)
> (*to* LADY CAPULET)
> How! doth she not give us thanks?
> Unworthy as she is, that we have wrought
> So worthy a gentleman to be her bridegroom?

JULIET *(standing up to* CAPULET*)*

> Proud can I never be of what I hate;

CAPULET

> What is this?
>> *(turns and approaches* JULIET *menacingly;*
>> *she shrinks away)*
>
> Fettle your fine joints 'gainst Thursday next,
> To go with Paris to Saint Peter's Church,
> Or I will drag thee on a hurdle thither.
> Out, you green-sickness carrion! out, you baggage!
> You tallow-face!
>> *(pulls his hand back as if to hit her)*

JULIET *(on her knees, almost weeping)*

> Good father, I beseech you on my knees,
> Hear me with patience but to speak a word.

CAPULET *(yelling)*

> Hang thee, young baggage! disobedient wretch!
> I tell thee what: get thee to church o' Thursday,
> Or never after look me in the face:
> Speak not, reply not, do not answer me;
> My fingers itch.
>> *(again makes hand motion as if to hit her,*
>> *then comes downstage center)*
>
> God's bread! it makes me mad:
> Day, night, hour, tide, time, work, play,
> Alone, in company, still my care hath been
> To have her match'd: and having now provided
> A gentleman of noble parentage,
> to have a wretched puling fool,
> answer 'I'll not wed';
> Graze where you will you shall not house with me:
> For, by my soul, I'll ne'er acknowledge thee.

CAPULET *exit stage rear*

JULIET *(still on the floor)*
> Is there no pity sitting in the clouds,
> That sees into the bottom of my grief?
> O, sweet my mother, cast me not away!
> *(holds arms outstretched)*

LADY CAPULET *(turns completely away)*
> Talk not to me, for I'll not speak a word:
> Do as thou wilt, for I have done with thee.

LADY CAPULET *exit stage rear.*

NURSE *comes up from behind* JULIET *and puts her arms around her, comfortingly.* JULIET *cries on her shoulder.*

JULIET
> O nurse, What say'st thou? hast thou not a word of joy?
> Some comfort, nurse.

NURSE *(turns to* JULIET *and helps her up on the bed; both sit,*
> JULIET *on right)*
> Faith, here it is.
> Romeo is banish'd; I think it best you married with
> the county.
> O, he's a lovely gentleman!

JULIET *(gets up from bed, facing downstage, not looking at* NURSE)
> Well, thou hast comforted me marvelous much.
> Go in: and tell my lady I am gone,
> Having displeased my father, to Laurence' cell,
> To make confession and to be absolved.

NURSE
> Marry, I will; and this is wisely done.

Exit NURSE *stage rear.*

JULIET
> I'll to the friar, to know his remedy:
> If all else fail, myself have power to die.

Exit JULIET *stage left.*

✳ **SCENE 4.** (ACT V, SCENE III)

A tomb.

NARRATOR

> Friar Lawrence has given Juliet a potion that will
> make her appear dead the morning of her planned
> wedding to Paris. Juliet's parents have laid her body
> in Capulet's tomb. Romeo thinks Juliet has died,
> and he buys poison so he can join her in death. At
> that same time, Paris visits Juliet's tomb.

JULIET *lies center stage on bench covered with a sheet.*

Enter **PARIS**, *with flowers, from stage right.*

PARIS

> Sweet flower, with flowers thy bridal bed I strew,—
> O woe! thy canopy is dust and stones;—
> Which with sweet water nightly I will dew,
> Or, wanting that, with tears distill'd by moans:
> > **THE PAGE** *whistles offstage*
> The boy gives warning something doth approach.
> What cursed foot wanders this way to-night,
> To cross my obsequies and true love's rite?
> What with a torch! muffle me, night, a while.

PARIS *hides behind stage right pillar.*

Enter **ROMEO** *and* **BALTHASAR**, *from stage left.*

ROMEO

> Why I descend into this bed of death,
> Is partly to behold my lady's face;
> therefore hence, be gone:
> But if thou, jealous, dost return to pry
> By heaven, I will tear thee joint by joint.

BALTHASAR

> I will be gone, sir, and not trouble you.
> *(aside)* For all this same, I'll hide me hereabout:
> His looks I fear, and his intents I doubt.

BALTHASAR *hides behind stage left pillar;* ROMEO *approaches the bench slowly;* PARIS *spies on* ROMEO.

> This is that banish'd haughty Montague,
> And here is come to do some villainous shame
> To the dead bodies: I will apprehend him.
> > *(comes forward)*
> Stop thy unhallow'd toil, vile Montague!
> Obey, and go with me; for thou must die.

ROMEO

> I must indeed; and therefore came I hither.
> Good gentle youth, tempt not a desperate man;
> Fly hence, and leave me:

PARIS

> I do defy thy conjurations,
> And apprehend thee for a felon here.

ROMEO

> Wilt thou provoke me? then have at thee, boy!
> > *(stabs* PARIS, *center stage)*

PARIS *(stumbles and falls, stage right)*
>O, I am slain!
>>*(falls, dies)*

ROMEO
>Let me peruse this face.
>Mercutio's kinsman, noble County Paris!
>Death, lie thou there, by a dead man interr'd.
>>*(sees JULIET)*
>Ah, dear Juliet,
>Why art thou yet so fair? O, here
>Will I set up my everlasting rest,
>And shake the yoke of inauspicious stars
>From this world-wearied flesh. Eyes, look your last!
>Arms, take your last embrace! and, lips, O you
>The doors of breath, seal with a righteous kiss
>A dateless bargain to engrossing death!
>Here's to my love!
>>*(drinks)*
>O true apothecary!
>Thy drugs are quick. Thus with a kiss I die.

ROMEO *goes to kiss* JULIET.
Dies in front of bench, just before he can get to her.

Enter FRIAR LAURENCE *from stage left.*

FRIAR LAURENCE
>Saint Francis be my speed! how oft to-night
>Have my old feet stumbled at graves!
>>*(sees BALTHASAR by stage left pillar)*
>Who's there?

BALTHASAR
>Here's one, a friend, and there's my master,
>One that you love.

FRIAR LAURENCE
> Who is it?

BALTHASAR
> Romeo.

FRIAR LAURENCE
> Go with me to the vault.

BALTHASAR
> I dare not, sir

FRIAR LAURENCE
> Stay, then; I'll go alone.

Exit BALTHASAR *stage rear.*

> Fear comes upon me:
> O, much I fear some ill unlucky thing.

FRIAR LAURENCE
> Romeo!
> > *(kneels, sees* PARIS'S *blood on* ROMEO*)*
> Alack, alack, what blood is this?
> Romeo! O, pale!
> > *(sees* PARIS *to right)*
> Who else? what, Paris too?
> And steep'd in blood? Ah, what an unkind hour
> Is guilty of this lamentable chance!
> > *(*JULIET *moves on bench)*
> The lady stirs.

JULIET *wakes.*

JULIET

> O comfortable friar! where is my lord?
> I do remember well where I should be,
> And there I am. Where is my Romeo?

FRIAR LAURENCE

> *(hears noise stage rear)*
> I hear some noise. Lady, come away.
> Thy husband in thy bosom there lies dead;
> *(hears noise again)*
> I dare no longer stay.

JULIET

> Go, get thee hence, for I will not away.

Exit **FRIAR LAURENCE** *stage right.*

> What's here? a cup, closed in my true love's hand?
> Poison, I see, hath been his timeless end:
> O churl! drunk all, and left no friendly drop
> To help me after? I will kiss thy lips;
> Haply some poison yet doth hang on them,
> To make die with a restorative.
> *(kisses him)*
> Thy lips are warm.
> *(hears noise stage rear)*

JULIET

> Yea, noise? then I'll be brief. O happy dagger!
> *(snatching* **ROMEO'S** *dagger)*
> This is thy sheath;
> *(stabs herself)*
> there rust, and let me die.
> *(falls on* **ROMEO'S** *body, and dies)*

Enter the **PRINCE** *from stage rear; also three citizens.*

PRINCE

What misadventure is so early up,
That calls our person from our morning's rest?

Enter CAPULET, LADY CAPULET, *three more citizens from stage right.*

The people in the street cry Romeo,
Some Juliet, and some Paris; and all run,
With open outcry toward our monument.
What fear is this which startles in our ears?
Search, seek, and know how this foul murder comes.

CAPULET

O heavens! O wife, look how our daughter bleeds!
This dagger hath mista'en—for, lo, his house
Is empty on the back of Montague,—
And it mis-sheathed in my daughter's bosom!

LADY CAPULET

O me! this sight of death is as a bell,
That warns my old age to a sepulchre.

Enter MONTAGUE *and three more citizens.*

Come, Montague; for thou art early up,
To see thy son and heir more early down.

MONTAGUE

Alas, my liege, my wife is dead tonight;
Grief of my son's exile hath stopp'd her breath:
What further woe conspires against mine age?

PRINCE

Look, and thou shalt see.
Bring forth the parties of suspicion.

FRIAR LAURENCE

> I am the greatest, able to do least,
> And here I stand, both to impeach and purge
> Myself condemned and myself excused.

PRINCE

> Then say at once what thou dost know in this.

FRIAR LAURENCE

> I will be brief,
> Romeo, there dead, was husband to that Juliet;
> And she, there dead, that Romeo's faithful wife:
> I married them; If aught in this
> Miscarried by my fault, let my old life
> Be sacrificed, some hour before his time,
> Unto the rigour of severest law.

PRINCE

> We still have known thee for a holy man.
> Capulet! Montague!
> See, what a scourge is laid upon your hate,
> That heaven finds means to kill your joys with love.
> And I for winking at your discords too
> Have lost a brace of kinsmen: all are punish'd.

CAPULET (to Montague)

> O brother Montague, give me thy hand:
> This is my daughter's jointure, for no more
> Can I demand.

The rest of the cast and crew enter, all forming a semicircle or line.

PRINCE

> A glooming peace this morning with it brings;
> The sun, for sorrow, will not show his head:

Go hence, to have more talk of these sad things;
Some shall be pardon'd, and some punished:

ALL TOGETHER:

For never was a story of more woe
Than this of Juliet and her Romeo.
All hold hands and take a bow. Exeunt.

STAGEHANDS ONE AND TWO *clear bench from stage.*

Return to seats amidst thunderous applause!

✳ PERFORMING SHAKESPEARE

BACKGROUND:
HOW *THE 30-MINUTE SHAKESPEARE* WAS BORN

In 1981 I performed a "Shakespeare Juggling" piece called "To Juggle or Not To Juggle" at the first Folger Library Secondary School Shakespeare Festival. The audience consisted of about 200 Washington, D.C. area high school students who had just performed thirty-minute versions of Shakespeare plays for each other and were jubilant over the experience. I was dressed in a jester's outfit, and my job was to entertain them. I juggled and jested and played with Shakespeare's words, notably Hamlet's "To be or not to be" soliloquy, to very enthusiastic response. I was struck by how much my "Shakespeare Juggling" resonated with a group who had just performed Shakespeare themselves. "Getting" Shakespeare is a heady feeling, especially for adolescents, and I am continually delighted at how much joy and satisfaction young people derive from performing Shakespeare. Simply reading and studying this great playwright does not even come close to inspiring the kind of enthusiasm that comes from performance.

Surprisingly, many of these students were not "actor types." A good percentage of the students performing Shakespeare that day were part of an English class which had rehearsed the plays during class time. Fifteen years later, when I first started directing plays in D.C. public schools as a Teaching Artist with the Folger Shakespeare Library, I entered a ninth grade English class as a guest and spent two or three days a week for two or three months preparing students for the Folger's annual Secondary School Shakespeare Festival. I have conducted this annual residency with the Folger ever since.

Every year for seven action-packed days, eight groups of students between grades seven and twelve tread the boards onstage at the Folger's Elizabethan Theatre, a grand recreation of a sixteenth-century venue with a three-tiered gallery, carved oak columns, and a sky-painted canopy.

As noted on the Folger website (www.folger.edu), "The festival is a celebration of the Bard, not a competition. Festival commentators—drawn from the professional theater and Shakespeare education communities—recognize exceptional performances, student directors, and good spirit amongst the students with selected awards at the end of each day. They are also available to share feedback with the students."

My annual Folger Teaching Artist engagement, directing a Shakespeare play in a public high school English class, is the most challenging and the most rewarding thing I do all year. I hope this book can bring you the same rewards.

GETTING STARTED: GAMES

How can you get an English class (or any other group of young people, or even adults) to start the seemingly daunting task of performing a Shakespeare play? You have already successfully completed the critical first step, which is buying this book. You hold in your hand a performance-ready, thirty-minute cutting of a Shakespeare play, with stage directions to get the actors moving about the stage purposefully. But it's a good idea to warm the group up with some theater games.

One good initial exercise is called "Positive/Negative Salutations." Students stand in two lines facing each other (four or five students in each line) and, reading from index cards, greet each other, first with a "Positive" salutation in Shakespeare's language (using actual phrases from the plays), followed by a "negative" greeting.

Additionally, short vocal exercises are an essential part of the preparation process. The following is a very simple and effective vocal warm-up: Beginning with the number two, have the whole group count to twenty using increments of two (i.e., "Two, four, six . . ."). Increase the volume slightly with each number, reaching top volume with "twenty," and then decrease the volume while counting back down, so that the students are practically whispering when they arrive again at "two." This exercise teaches dynamics and allows them to get loud as a group without any individual pressure. Frequently during a rehearsal period, if a student is mumbling inaudibly, I will refer back to this exercise as a reminder that we can and often do belt it out!

"Stomping Words" is a game that is very helpful at getting a handle on Shakespeare's rhythm. Choose a passage in iambic pentameter and have the group members walk around the room in a circle, stomping their feet on the second beat of each line:

Two **house**-holds, **both** a-**like** in **dig**-nity
In **fair** Ve-**ro**na **Where** we **lay** our **scene**

Do the same thing with a prose passage, and have the students discuss their experience with it, including points at which there is an extra beat, etc., and what, if anything, it might signify.

I end every vocal warm-up with a group reading of one of the speeches from the play, emphasizing diction and projection, bouncing off consonants, and encouraging the group members to listen to each other so that they can speak the lines together in unison. For variety I will throw in some classic "tongue twisters" too, such as, "The sixth sheik's sixth sheep is sick."

The Folger Shakespeare Library's website (http://www.folger.edu) and their book series *Shakespeare Set Free*, edited by Peggy O'Brien, are two great resources for getting started with a performance-based teaching of Shakespeare in the classroom. The Folger website has numerous helpful resources and activities, many submitted by teachers, for helping a class actively participate in the process of getting to know a Shakespeare play. For more simple theater games, Viola Spolin's *Theatre Games for the Classroom* is very helpful, as is one I use frequently, *Theatre Games for Young Performers.*

HATS AND PROPS

Introducing a few hats and props early in the process is a good way to get the action going. Hats, in particular, provide a nice avenue for giving young actors a non-verbal way of getting into character. In the opening weeks, when students are still holding onto their scripts, a hat can give an actor a way to "feel" like a character. Young actors are natural masters at injecting their own personality into what they wear, and even small choices made with how a hat is worn (jauntily, shadily, cockily, mysteriously) provide a starting point for discussion of specific characters, their traits, and their relationships with other characters. All such discussions always lead back to one thing: the text. "Mining the text" is consistently the best strategy for uncovering the mystery of Shakespeare's language. That is where all the answers lie: in the words themselves.

WHAT DO THE WORDS MEAN?

It is essential that young actors know what they are saying when they recite Shakespeare. If not, they might as well be scat singing, riffing on sounds and rhythm but not conveying a specific meaning. The real question is: What do the words mean? The answer is multifaceted, and can be found in more than one place. The New Folger Library paperback editions of the plays themselves (edited by Barbara Mowat and Paul Werstine, Washington Square Press) are a great resource for understanding Shakespeare's words and passages and "translating" them into modern English. These editions also contain chapters on Shakespeare's language, his life, his theater, a "Modern Perspective," and further reading. There is a wealth of scholarship embedded in these wonderful books, and I make it a point to read them cover to cover before embarking on a play-directing project. At the very least, it is a good idea for any adult who intends to direct a Shakespeare play with a group of students to go through the explanatory notes that appear on the pages facing the text. These explanatory notes are an indispensable "translation tool."

The best way to get students to understand what Shakespeare's words mean is to ask them what they think they mean. Students have their own associations with the words and with how they sound and feel. The best ideas on how to perform Shakespeare often come directly from the students, not from anybody else's notion. If a student has an idea or feeling about a word or passage, and it resonates with her emotionally, physically, or spiritually, then Shakespeare's words can be a vehicle for her feelings. That can result in some powerful performances!

I make it my job as director to read the explanatory notes in the Folger text, but I make it clear to the students that almost "anything goes" when trying to understand Shakespeare. There are no wrong interpretations. Students have their own experiences, with some shared and some uniquely their own. If someone has an association with the phrase "canker-blossom," or if the words make that student or his character feel or act a certain way, then that is the "right" way to decipher it.

I encourage the students to refer to the Folger text's explanatory notes and to keep a pocket dictionary handy. Young actors must attach some meaning to every word or line they recite. If I feel an actor is glossing over a word, I will stop him and ask him what he is saying. If he doesn't know, we will figure it out together as a group.

PROCESS VS. PRODUCT

The process of learning Shakespeare by performing one of his plays is more important than whether everybody remembers his lines or whether somebody misses a cue or an entrance. But my Teaching Artist residencies have always had the end goal of a public performance for about 200 other students, so naturally the performance starts to take precedence over the process somewhere around Dress Rehearsal in the students' minds. It is my job to make sure the actors are prepared—otherwise they will remember the embarrassing moment of a public mistake and not the glorious triumph of owning a Shakespeare play.

In one of my earlier years of play directing, I was sitting in the audience as one of my narrators stood frozen on stage for at least a minute, trying to remember her opening line. I started scrambling in my backpack below my seat for a script, at last prompting her from the audience. Despite her fine performance, that embarrassing moment is all she remembered from the whole experience. Since then I have made sure to assign at least one person to prompt from backstage if necessary. Additionally, I inform the entire cast that if somebody is dying alone out there, it is okay to rescue him or her with an offstage prompt.

There is always a certain amount of stage fright that will accompany a performance, especially a public one for an unfamiliar audience. As a director, I live with stage fright as well, even though I am not appearing on stage. The only antidote to this is work and preparation. If a young actor is struggling with her lines, I make sure to arrange for a session where we run lines over the telephone. I try to set up a buddy system so that students can run lines with their peers, and this often works well. But if somebody does not have a "buddy," I will personally make the time to help out myself. As I assure my students from the outset, I am not going to let them fail or embarrass themselves. They need an experienced leader. And if the leader has experience in teaching but not in directing Shakespeare, then he needs this book!

It is a good idea to culminate in a public performance, as opposed to an in-class project, even if it is only for another classroom. Student actors want to show their newfound Shakespearian thespian skills to an outside group, and this goal motivates them to do a good job. In that respect, "product" is important. Another wonderful bonus to performing a play is that it is a unifying group effort. Students learn teamwork. They learn to give focus to another actor when he is speaking, and to play off of other characters. I like to end each performance with the entire cast reciting a passage in unison. This is a powerful ending, one that reaffirms the unity of the group.

SEEING SHAKESPEARE PERFORMED

It is very helpful for young actors to see Shakespeare performed by a group of professionals, whether they are appearing live on stage (preferable but not always possible) or on film. Because an entire play can take up two or more full class periods, time may be an issue. I am fortunate because thanks to a local foundation that underwrites theater education in the schools, I have been able to take my school groups to a Folger Theatre matinee of the play that they are performing. I always pick a play that is being performed locally that season. But not all group leaders are that lucky. Fortunately, there is the Internet, specifically YouTube. A quick YouTube search for "Shakespeare" can unearth thousands of results, many appropriate for the classroom.

The first "Hamlet" result showed an 18-year-old African-American actor on the streets of Camden, New Jersey, delivering a riveting performance of Hamlet's "The play's the thing." The second clip was from *Cat Head Theatre,* an animation of cats performing Hamlet. Of course, YouTube boasts not just alley cats and feline thespians, but also clips by true legends of the stage, such as John Gielgud and Richard Burton. These clips can be saved and shown in classrooms, providing useful inspiration.

One advantage of the amazing variety of clips available on YouTube is that students can witness the wide range of interpretations for any given scene, speech, or character in Shakespeare, thus freeing them from any preconceived notion that there is a "right" way to do it.

Furthermore, modern interpretations of the Bard may appeal to those who are put off by the "thees and thous" of Elizabethan speech.

By seeing Shakespeare performed either live or on film, students are able to hear the cadence, rhythm, vocal dynamics, and pronunciation of the language, and they can appreciate the life that other actors breathe into the characters. They get to see the story told dramatically, which inspires them to tell their own version.

PUTTING IT ALL TOGETHER: THE STEPS

After a few sessions of theater games to warm up the group, it's time to begin the process of casting the play. Each play cutting in *The 30-Minute Shakespeare* series includes a cast list and a sample program, demonstrating which parts have been divided. Cast size is generally between twenty and thirty students, with major roles frequently assigned to more than one performer. In other words, one student may play Juliet in the first scene, another in the second scene, and yet another in the third. This will distribute the parts evenly so that there is no "star of the show." Furthermore, this prevents actors from being burdened with too many lines. If I have an actor who is particularly talented or enthusiastic, I will give her a bigger role. It is important to go with the grain—one cast member's enthusiasm can be contagious.

I provide the performer of each shared role with a similar headpiece and/or cape, so that the audience can keep track of the characters. When there are sets of twins, I try to use blue shirts and red shirts, so that the audience has at least a fighting chance of figuring it out! Other than these costume consistencies, I rely on the text and the audience's observance to sort out the doubling of characters. Generally, the audience can follow because we are telling the story.

Some participants are shy and do not wish to speak at all on stage. To these students I assign non-speaking parts and technical roles such as sound operator and stage manager. However, I always get everybody on stage at some point, even if it is just for the final group speech, because I want every group member to experience what it is like to be on a stage as part of an ensemble.

CASTING THE PLAY

Young people can be self-conscious and nervous with "formal" auditions, especially if they have little or no acting experience.

I conduct what I call an "informal" audition process. I hand out a questionnaire asking students if there is any particular role that they desire, whether they play a musical instrument. To get a feel for them as people, I also ask them to list one or two hobbies or interests. Occasionally this will inform my casting decisions. If someone can juggle, and the play has the part of a Fool, that skill may come in handy. Dancing or martial arts abilities can also be applied to roles.

For the auditions, I do not use the cut script. I have students stand and read from the Folger edition of the complete text in order to hear how they fare with the longer passages. I encourage them to breathe and carry their vocal energy all the way to the end of a long line of text. I also urge them to play with diction, projection, modulation, and dynamics, elements of speech that we have worked on in our vocal warm-ups and theater games.

I base my casting choices largely on reading ability, vocal strength, and enthusiasm for the project. If someone has requested a particular role, I try to honor that request. I explain that even with a small part, an actor can create a vivid character that adds a lot to the play. Wide variations in personality types can be utilized: if there are two students cast as Romeo, one brooding and one effusive, I try to put the more brooding Romeo in an early lovelorn scene, and place the effusive Romeo in the balcony scene. Occasionally one gets lucky, and the doubling of characters provides a way to match personality types with different aspects of a character's personality. But also be aware of the potential serendipity of non-traditional casting. For example,

I have had one of the smallest students in the class play a powerful Othello. True power comes from within!

Generally, I have more females than males in a class, so women are more likely (and more willing) to play male characters than vice versa. Rare is the high school boy who is brave enough to play a female character, which is unfortunate because it can reap hilarious results.

GET OUTSIDE HELP

Every time there is a fight scene in one of the plays I am directing, I call on my friend Michael Tolaydo, a professional actor and theater professor at St. Mary's College, who is an expert in all aspects of theater, including fight choreography. Not only does Michael stage the fight, but he does so in a way that furthers the action of the play, highlighting character's traits and bringing out the best in the student actors. Fight choreography must be done by an expert or somebody could get hurt. In the absence of such help, super slow-motion fights are always a safe bet and can be quite effective, especially when accompanied by a soundtrack on the boom box.

During dress rehearsals I invite my friend Hilary Kacser. a Washington-area actor and dialect coach for two decades. Because I bring her in late in the rehearsal process, I have her direct her comments to me, which I then filter and relay to the cast. This avoids confusing the cast with a second set of directions. This caveat only applies to general directorial comments from outside visitors. Comments on specific artistic disciplines such as dance, music, and stage combat can come from the outside experts themselves.

If you work in a school, you might have helpful resources within your own building, such as a music or dance teacher who could contribute their expertise to a scene. If nobody is available in your school, try seeking out a member of the local professional theater. Many local performing artists will be glad to help, and the students are usually thrilled to have a visit from a professional performer.

LET STUDENTS BRING THEMSELVES INTO THE PLAY

The best ideas often come from the students themselves. If a young actor has a notion of how to play a scene, I will always give that idea a try. In a rehearsal of *Henry IV, Part 1*, one traveler jumped into the other's arms when they were robbed. It got a huge laugh. This was something that they did on instinct. We kept that bit for the performance, and it worked wonderfully.

As a director, you have to foster an environment in which that kind of spontaneity can occur. The students have to feel safe to experiment. In the same production of *Henry IV*, Falstaff and Hal invented a little fist bump "secret handshake" to use in the battle scene. The students were having fun and bringing parts of themselves into the play. Shakespeare himself would have approved. When possible I try to err on the side of fun because if the young actors are having fun, then they will commit themselves to the project. The beauty of the language, the story, the characters, and the pathos will follow.

There is a balance to be achieved here, however. In that same production of *Henry IV, Part 1*, the student who played Bardolph was having a great time with her character. She carried a leather wineskin around and offered it up to the other characters in the tavern. It was a prop with which she developed a comic relationship. At the end of our thirty-minute *Henry IV, Part 1*, I added a scene from *Henry IV, Part 2* as a coda: The new King Henry V (formerly Falstaff's drinking and carousing buddy Hal) rejects Falstaff, banishing him from within ten miles of the King. It is a sad and sobering moment, one of the most powerful in the play.

But at the performance, in the middle of the King's rejection speech (played by a female student, and her only speech), Bardolph offered her flask to King Henry and got a big laugh, thus not only upstaging the King but also undermining the seriousness and poignancy of the whole scene. She did not know any better; she was bringing herself to the character as I had been encouraging her to do. But it was inappropriate, and in subsequent seasons, if I foresaw something like that happening as an individual joyfully occupied a character, I attempted to prevent it. Some things we cannot predict. Now I make sure to issue a statement warning against changing any of the blocking on show day, and to watch out for upstaging one's peers.

FOUR FORMS OF ENGAGEMENT: VOCAL, EMOTIONAL, PHYSICAL, AND INTELLECTUAL

When directing a Shakespeare play with a group of students, I always start with the words themselves because the words have the power to engage the emotions, mind, and body. Also, I start with the words in action, as in the previously mentioned exercise, "Positive and Negative Salutations." Students become physically engaged; their bodies react to the images the words evoke. The words have the power to trigger a switch in both the teller and the listener, eliciting both an emotional and physical reaction. I have never heard a student utter the line "Fie! Fie! You counterfeit, you puppet you!" without seeing him change before my eyes. His spine stiffens, his eyes widen, and his fingers point menacingly.

Having used Shakespeare's words to engage the students emotionally and physically, one can then return to the text for a more reflective discussion of what the words mean to us personally. I always make sure to leave at least a few class periods open for discussion of the text, line by line, to ensure that students understand intellectually what they feel viscerally. The advantage to a performance-based teaching of Shakespeare is that by engaging students vocally, emotionally, and physically, it is then much easier to engage them intellectually because they are invested in the words, the characters, and the story. We always start on our feet, and later we sit and talk.

SIX ELEMENTS OF DRAMA: PLOT, CHARACTER, THEME, DICTION, MUSIC, AND SPECTACLE

Over two thousand years ago, Aristotle's *Poetics* outlined six elements of drama, in order of importance: Plot, Character, Theme, Diction, Music, and Spectacle. Because Shakespeare was foremost a playwright, it is helpful to take a brief look at these six elements as they relate to directing a Shakespeare play in the classroom.

PLOT (ACTION)

To Aristotle, plot was the most important element. One of the purposes of *The 30-Minute Shakespeare* is to provide a script that tells Shakespeare's stories, as opposed to concentrating on one scene. In a thirty-minute edit of a Shakespeare play, some plot elements are necessarily omitted. For the sake of a full understanding of the characters' relationships and motivations, it is helpful to make short plot summaries of each scene so that students are aware of their characters' arcs throughout the play. The scene descriptions in the Folger editions are sufficient to fill in the plot holes. Students can read the descriptions aloud during class time to ensure that the story is clear and that no plot elements are neglected. Additionally, there are one-page charts in the Folger editions of *Shakespeare Set Free,* indicating characters' relations graphically, with lines connecting families and factions to give students a visual representation of what can often be complex interrelationships, particularly in Shakespeare's history plays.

Young actors love action. That is why *The 30-Minute Shakespeare* includes dynamic blocking (stage direction) that allows students to tell the story in a physically dramatic fashion. Characters' movements on the stage are always motivated by the text itself.

CHARACTER

I consider myself a facilitator and a director more than an acting teacher. I want the students' understanding of their characters to spring from the text and the story. From there, I encourage them to consider how their character might talk, walk, stand, sit, eat, and drink. I also urge students to consider characters' motivations, objectives, and relationships, and I will ask pointed questions to that end during the rehearsal process. I try not to show the students how I would perform a scene, but if no ideas are forthcoming from anybody in the class, I will suggest a minimum of two possibilities for how the character might respond.

At times students may want more guidance and examples. Over thirteen years of directing plays in the classroom, I have wavered between wanting all the ideas to come from the students, and deciding that I need to be more of a "director," telling them what I would like to see them doing. It is a fine line, but in recent years I have decided that if I don't see enough dynamic action or characterization, I will step in and "direct" more. But I always make sure to leave room for students to bring themselves into the characters because their own ideas are invariably the best.

THEME (THOUGHTS, IDEAS)

In a typical English classroom, theme will be a big topic for discussion of a Shakespeare play. Using a performance-based method of teaching Shakespeare, an understanding of the play's themes develops from "mining the text" and exploring Shakespeare's words and his story. If the students understand what they are saying and how that relates to their characters and the overall story, the plays' themes will emerge clearly. We always return to the text itself. There are a number of elegant computer programs, such as www.wordle.net, that will count the number of recurring words in a passage and illustrate them graphically. For example, if the word "jealousy" comes up more than any other word in *Othello,* it will appear in a larger font. Seeing the words displayed by size in this way can offer up illuminating insights into the interaction between words in the text and the play's themes. Your computer-minded students might enjoy searching for such tidbits. There are more internet tools and websites in the Additional Resources section at the back of this book.

I cannot overstress the importance of acting out the play in understanding its themes. By embodying the roles of Othello and Iago and reciting their words, students do not simply comprehend the themes intellectually, but understand them kinesthetically, physically, and emotionally. They are essentially **living** the characters' jealousy, pride, and feelings about race. The themes of appearance vs. reality, good vs. evil, honesty, misrepresentation, and self-knowledge (or lack thereof) become physically felt as well as intellectually understood. Performing Shakespeare delivers a richer understanding than that which comes from just reading the play. Students can now relate the characters' conflicts to their own struggles.

DICTION (LANGUAGE)

If I had to cite one thing I would like my actors to take from their experience of performing a play by William Shakespeare, it is an appreciation and understanding of the beauty of Shakespeare's language. The language is where it all begins and ends. Shakespeare's stories are dramatic, his characters are rich and complex, and his settings are exotic and fascinating, but it is through his language that these all achieve their richness. This leads me to spend more time on language than on any other element of the performance.

Starting with daily vocal warm-ups, many of them using parts of the script or other Shakespearean passages, I consistently emphasize the importance of the words. Young actors often lack experience in speaking clearly and projecting their voices outward, so in addition to comprehension, I emphasize projection, diction, breathing, pacing, dynamics, coloring of words, and vocal energy. *Theatre Games for Young Performers* contains many effective vocal exercises, as does the Folger's *Shakespeare Set Free* series. Consistent emphasis on all aspects of Shakespeare's language, especially on how to speak it effectively, is the most important element to any Shakespeare performance with a young cast.

MUSIC

A little music can go a long way in setting a mood for a thirty-minute Shakespeare play. I usually open the show with a short passage of music to set the tone. Thirty seconds of music played on a boom box operated by a student can provide a nice introduction to the play, create an atmosphere for the audience, and give the actors a sense of place and feeling.

iTunes is a good starting point for choosing your music. Typing in "Shakespeare" or "Hamlet" or "jealousy" (if you are going for a theme) will result in an excellent selection of aural performance enhancers at the very reasonable price of ninety-nine cents each (or free of charge, see Additional Resources section.) Likewise, fight sounds, foreboding sounds, weather sounds (rain, thunder), trumpet sounds, etc. are all readily available online at affordable cost. I typically include three sound cues in a play, just enough to enhance but not overpower a production. The boom box operator sits on the far right or left of the stage, not backstage, so he can see the action. This also has the added benefit of having somebody out there with a script, capable of prompting in a pinch.

SPECTACLE

Aristotle considered spectacle the least important aspect of drama. Students tend to be surprised at this since we are used to being bombarded with production values on TV and video, often at the expense of substance. In my early days of putting on student productions, I would find myself hamstrung by my own ambitions in the realm of scenic design.

A simple bench or two chairs set on the stage are sufficient. The sense of "place" can be achieved through language and acting. Simple set dressing, a few key props, and some tasteful, emblematic costume pieces will go a long way toward providing all the "spectacle" you need.

In the stage directions to the plays in *The 30-Minute Shakespeare* series, I make frequent use of two large pillars stage left and right at the Folger Shakespeare Library's Elizabethan Theatre. I also have characters frequently entering and exiting from "stage rear." Your stage will have a different layout. Take a good look at the performing space you will be using and see if there are any elements that can be incorporated into your own stage directions. Is there a balcony? Can characters enter from the audience? (Make sure that they can get there from backstage, unless you want them waiting in the lobby until their entrance, which may be impractical.) If possible, make sure to rehearse in that space a few times to fix any technical issues and perhaps discover a few fun staging variations that will add pizzazz and dynamics to your own show.

The real spectacle is in the telling of the tale. Wooden swords are handy for characters that need them. Students should be warned at the outset that playing with swords outside of the scene is verboten. Letters, moneybags, and handkerchiefs should all have plentiful duplicates kept in a small prop box, as well as with a stage manager, because they tend to disappear in the hands of adolescents. After every rehearsal and performance, I recommend you personally sweep the rehearsal or performance area immediately for stray props. It is amazing what gets left behind.

Ultimately, the performances are about language and human drama, not set pieces, props, and special effects. Fake blood, glitter, glass, and liquids have no place on the stage; they are a recipe for disaster, or, at the very least, a big mess. On the other hand, the props that are employed can often be used effectively to convey character, as in Bardolph's aforementioned relationship with his wineskin.

PITFALLS AND SOLUTIONS

Putting on a play in a high school classroom is not easy. There are problems with enthusiasm, attitude, attention, and line memorization, to name a few. As anybody who has directed a play will tell you, it is always darkest before the dawn. My experience is that after one or two days of utter despair just before the play goes up, show day breaks and the play miraculously shines. To quote a recurring gag in one of my favorite movies, *Shakespeare in Love:* "It's a mystery."

ENTHUSIASM, FRUSTRATION, AND DISCIPLINE

Bring the enthusiasm yourself. Feed on the energy of the eager students, and others will pick up on that. Keep focused on the task at hand. Arrive prepared. Enthusiasm comes as you make headway. Ultimately, it helps to remind the students that a "play" is fun. I try to focus on the positive attributes of the students, rather than the ones that drive me crazy. This is easier said than done, but it is important. One season, I yelled at the group two days in a row. On day two of yelling, they tuned me out, and it took me a while to win them back. I learned my lesson; since then I've tried not to raise my voice out of anger or frustration. As I grow older and more mature, it is important for me to lead by example. It has been years since I yelled at a student group. If I am disappointed in their work or their behavior, I will express my disenchantment in words, speaking from the heart as somebody who cares about them and cares about our performance and our experience together. I find that fundamentally, young people want to please, to do well, and to be liked. If there is a serious discipline problem, I will hand it over to the regular classroom teacher, the administrator, or the parent.

LINE MEMORIZATION

Students may have a hard time memorizing lines. In these cases, see if you can pair them up with a "buddy" and existing friend who will run lines with them in person or over the phone after school. If students do not have such a "buddy," I volunteer to run lines with them myself. If serious line memorization problems arise that cannot be solved through work, then two students can switch parts if it is early enough in the rehearsal process. For doubled roles, the scene with fewer lines can go to the actor who is having memorization problems. Additionally, a few passages or lines can be cut. Again, it is important to address these issues early. Later cuts become more problematic as other actors have already memorized their cues. I have had to do late cuts about twice in thirteen years. While they have gotten us out of jams, it is best to assess early whether a student will have line memorization problems, and deal with the problem sooner rather than later.

In production, always keep several copies of the script backstage, as well as cheat sheets indicating cues, entrances, and scene changes. Make a prop list, indicating props for each scene, as well as props that are the responsibility of individual actors. Direct the Stage Manager and an Assistant Stage Manager to keep track of these items, and on show days, personally double-check if you can.

In thirteen years of preparing an inner-city public high school English class for a public performance on a field trip to the Folger Secondary School Shakespeare Festival, my groups and I have been beset by illness, emotional turmoil, discipline problems, stage fright, adolescent angst, midlife crises (not theirs), and all manner of other emergencies, including acts of God and nature. Despite the difficulties and challenges inherent in putting on a Shakespeare play with a group of young people, one amazing fact stands out in my experience. Here is how many times a student has been absent for show day: Zero. Somehow, everybody has always made it to the show, and the show has gone on. How can this be? It's a mystery.

✳ PERFORMANCE NOTES: *ROMEO AND JULIET*

I directed this production of *Romeo and Juliet* in 2005 with a ninth grade English class. It was a challenging and rewarding season for me. I had some discipline issues that year. I had the impression that my students were pushing me, or testing me, and I yelled at them two days in a row during the rehearsal period, which backfired a bit because it took some of the fun out of the process. I later apologized for it, and we eventually got back on track and started having fun with the play again, resulting in a lively and satisfying performance from the group. That was a learning experience for me, and in subsequent years I have refrained from raising my voice in that way. It is possible that I had some growing up to do, too.

These notes are the result of my own review of the performance video. They are not intended to be the "definitive" performance notes for all productions of *Romeo and Juliet*. Your production will be unique to you and your cast. That is the magic of live theater. What is interesting about these notes is that many of the performance details I mention were not part of the original stage directions. They either emerged spontaneously on performance day or were developed by students in rehearsal after the stage directions had been written into the script. Some of these pieces of stage business work like a charm. Others fall flat. Still others are unintentionally hilarious. My favorites are the ones that arise directly from the students themselves, and demonstrate a union between actor and character, as if that individual becomes a vehicle for the character she is playing. To witness a fifteen-year-old girl "become" Juliet as Shakespeare's words leave her mouth is a memorable moment indeed.

While directing Scene Three (III.5), during which Lord Capulet yells at Juliet for disobeying his directive that she should marry Paris, I suggest to the actor playing Capulet that he pretend he is Mr. Newlin yelling at the class. There are times when art can indeed imitate life. Ninth graders have rich emotional lives (as do teachers), so *Romeo and Juliet* is a play they can sink their teeth into. Playing a tragedy is tricky because with adolescents, comedy is never very far away. The most memorable moment in this production of *Romeo and Juliet* comes in Scene Four (V.3), the final scene at the tomb. I had mentioned to the student playing Lady Capulet that it was okay to cry at Juliet's tomb. What I was not prepared for was what she chose to do instead: She let out a piercing, high-pitched shriek, cried, "My baby!" at the top of her lungs, and slid on her knees with her arms outstretched to dead Juliet's side, to sidesplitting extended laughter from the audience. So much for tragedy. After that incident, I made it a policy to implement stern warnings about "experimenting" with alternate interpretations on show day. The experimentation should take place during the rehearsal process, not performances.

The following comments are the result of reviewing a DVD of my ninth grade group's performance of *Romeo* at the Folger Library Secondary School Shakespeare Festival. A video camera mounted on a tripod is one of the best study tools around. Watching a DVD of the rehearsal or show frequently unearths small details that are missed the first time around.

SCENE 1 (ACT I, SCENE I)

Foreboding opening music played on the boom box sets a good tone for a tragedy and puts both actors and audience on alert for bad things ahead. As the music plays, the character performing the Prologue walks slowly downstage and stops, delivering the prologue in its entirety with no cuts. The Prologue should not be rushed. Be aware of "beats," or pauses between words or phrases that allow the language to sink in. Small gestures such as crossing the hands over the heart during the phrase "two star-crossed lovers" provide an effective physical representation of the words. Small physical gestures can go a long way toward reinforcing linguistic images.

In the opening meeting between the Capulets (Sampson and Gregory) and Montagues (Abraham and Balthasar), both couples should stay at either end of the stage initially, leaving enough space between them to indicate caution and mistrust. When Benvolio and Tybalt enter, and the slow-motion fight breaks out, the actors should be moving extremely slowly with music behind them. The tendency will be for them to speed up the action, but super-slow motion is most effective for the fight. As soon as the Prince enters, all the actors should freeze, and the fighters should back up and bow at normal speed. When Benvolio describes the fight to Lord and Lady Montague, he should relive the action, demonstrating the fight with his sword.

SCENE 2 (ACT II, SCENE II)

It is always gratifying when a young actor brings herself to a role with enthusiasm and creates an indelible portrait of a character. So it was with the young lady who played Juliet in this 2005 production. In the balcony scene before Romeo's entrance, she stood on a bench (representing the balcony) and swung her arms from side to side, casually playing with her dress. This physicalization pointed toward Juliet's childlike, innocent side. A few moments later, Romeo startles Juliet from behind with the line, "I take thee at thy word." Rather than screaming, and almost falling into Romeo's arms as the stage directions suggested, the actress playing Juliet instead screamed, turned, and started hitting Romeo with her headpiece.

There are three reasons why I prefer this interpretation: 1) It arose from the actress herself, 2) It paints a more empowering portrait of the character of Juliet than falling into Romeo's arms would have, and 3) It is funny, and in performance, it gets a big laugh from the audience. Throughout the scene, the student playing Juliet brought herself to the character, repeatedly turning her back to Romeo and crossing her arms saucily, creating a nice comic tension. When Juliet says "Goodnight" three times to Romeo, this Juliet added a "Woo!" and did a running slide toward him on the bench. Then she gave Romeo a firm chuck on the chin before sashaying off the stage.

Who can resist such a Juliet? None of these moments were included in my stage directions. If I had the secret on how to elicit this kind of enthusiasm and creativity from a student actor, I would share it with you. If you foster an atmosphere of fun, and mine the text with the group for clues to what gives the character life, then anything is possible when performing Shakespeare with young actors.

SCENE 3 (ACT III, SCENE V)

Keep the bench in the same location for the final three scenes of the play, and use it to represent a balcony, a bed, and a tomb. Place a sheet and a pillow on the bench for Scene Two, and then remove them for Scene Three. This is an example of how minimal scene changes can nonetheless convey different locations. It took me years to curtail my desire to change the furniture for each scene. Unnecessary scene changes slow down the production and contribute to directorial frustration, since students are constitutionally averse to furniture moving. Some scene changes are necessary, but the fewer the better.

Romeo and Juliet kiss in this scene, as well as in the final scene. There are some issues surrounding kissing. I had tried to get a feel for this by asking on the questionnaire if the student would be willing to kiss another student in the play (with some hilarious responses). The issue was not whether the students were willing to kiss (they were)—the issue was the parents. Several parents were unhappy with the idea of their sons and daughters kissing on stage. (Parents apparently had no problem with theatrical depictions of murder and suicide.) We circumvented the issue by having students turn their heads and kiss on the cheek, while making it look like they were kissing on the lips. In the heat of the performance, students basically made their own decisions, and it looked real enough to me!

Little gestures in this dramatic scene can go a long way toward painting a visual picture of the relationships between characters. Upon entering and seeing Juliet weeping, Lady Capulet can reach out her hand to hold Juliet's hand. Similar choices can be made in Juliet's exchanges with the Nurse and Lord Capulet. Experiment with different potential responses by Juliet to see which resonates most with you and the actors. Juliet can pull her hand away. Juliet can hold her mother's hand but not maintain eye contact. Juliet can cry into her mother's arms. Each moment in a scene offers the actor and director a choice on how to speak the lines, which words to stress, and how to physicalize the interchange. Experiment with the options to give yourself a rich palette from which to paint the picture of the play.

SCENE 4 (ACT V, SCENE III)

As mentioned, playing tragedy with adolescents can be tricky. They are just as apt to laugh as to cry. Small details in how the lines are said or how bodies move can result in unintended laughter. During this final scene in my 2005 production of *Romeo and Juliet,* Romeo and Paris, once dead, are not able to stay still. For some reason, dead Romeo does not want to lie too close to dead Paris, so he keeps inching his body away from Paris, which tickles the audience's funny bone.

I have already mentioned the dramatic "My baby!" uttered by a screaming Lady Capulet in this scene, which also results in uproarious laughter from the audience in a scene where I would have preferred audience tears. But this is a ninth grade English class. Ultimately, I am glad the actors are committing to their performances.

At the Folger Library Secondary School Shakespeare Festival, students only perform the play once. There are no second chances. If you are fortunate enough to be able to mount the play for several shows, then what goes awry in the first performance can be fixed for the second. Use a video camera to capture all the details that you might miss, and then deliver specific notes that point out positive aspects of the students' work while suggesting ways they might improve.

Live theater is magical. It is the most dynamic form of entertainment available to us. There is nothing like the interchange between actors and audience, that vibrant energy that is created in the theater. *Romeo and Juliet* is surely one of the most powerful and enduring dramas ever written, and we are fortunate to be able to continue giving it life, especially with young performers who can give it the vitality it deserves.

✳ *ROMEO AND JULIET:*
SET AND PROP LIST

SET PIECES:

One bench

PROPS:

SCENE 1:
Boombox, cassette (or cd) or iPod with sound cues 1 and 2.
Various swords for Montagues and Capulets

SCENE 2:
Sheet and Pillow for bench (bed). Stagehands 1 and 2 place sheet
and pillow on bench at end of Scene 2. Before scene 2, Juliet
should have a ring on her person, to give to Romeo.

SCENE 4:
Flowers for Paris
1 Dagger, for Romeo, later taken by Juliet
1 vial of poison for Romeo

BENJAMIN BANNEKER ACADEMIC HIGH SCHOOL *presents*

Romeo and Juliet
By William Shakespeare

Folger Secondary School Shakespeare Festival | Tuesday, March 15th, 2005
9th Grade English Class | Instructor: Ms. Amina Brown
Guest Director: Mr. Nick Newlin

CAST OF CHARACTERS:

SCENE 1 (ACT I, SCENE I)

Verona, a public place

Prologue: Ivory Sherman
Sampson: Ranelle Grayton
Gregory: Monét Ray
Abraham: Alexis Turner
Balthasar: Jasmine Wilson
Benvolio: Alesia Ashley
Romeo: Shay Watkins
Tybalt: Ariel Grant
First Citizen: Shané Hughes
Capulet: Ruth Gebru
Lady Capulet: Jaleesa McCullough
Montague: Estefani Aria-Berrios
Lady Montague: Shaunté Canty
Prince: Maya Jumper
Brawling Montagues: William R. Dixon II, Emmanuel McCain

SCENE 2 (ACT II, SCENE II)

Capulet's Garden

Narrator: Monét Ray
Romeo: Zak Rogoff
Juliet: Ivory Sherman
Nurse (offstage voice): Leila Pree

Special Thanks:
Michael Tolaydo
Leo Bowman

SCENE 3 (ACT III, SCENE V)

Capulet's Home

Narrator: Mia Oliver
Romeo: William R. Dixon II
Juliet: Leila Pree
Nurse: Anaia Peddie
Lady Capulet: Kiersten Magee
Capulet: Honesty Eyo

SCENE 4 (ACT V, SCENE III)

A Tomb

Narrator: Anaia Peddie
Paris: Muhammad Mack
Romeo: Emmanuel McCain
Balthasar: Jasmine Wilson
Juliet: Chyna Terrell
Friar Laurence: Nathan Acors
Prince: Maya Jumper
Lady Capulet: Mia Oliver
Capulet: Honesty Eyo
Montague: Estefani Aria-Berrios

Stage Managers: Mia Oliver, Emmanuel McCain, Monét Ray
Scene Changes: Muhammad Mack, Emmanuel McCain
Costumes: Shaunté Canty
Props: Shané Hughes
Technical Director: Nathan Acors

*'Tis but thy name that is my enemy;
Thou art thyself, though not a Montague.
What's in a name? That which we call a rose
By any other name would smell as sweet.*
—Juliet

ADDITIONAL RESOURCES

SHAKESPEARE

Shakespeare Set Free: Teaching Romeo and Juliet, Macbeth and a Midsummer Night's Dream
Peggy O'Brien, Ed., Teaching Shakespeare Institute
Washington Square Press
New York, 1993

Shakespeare Set Free: Teaching Hamlet and Henry IV, Part 1
Peggy O'Brien, Ed., Teaching Shakespeare Institute
Washington Square Press
New York, 1994

Shakespeare Set Free: Teaching Twelfth Night and Othello
Peggy O'Brien, Ed., Teaching Shakespeare Institute
Washington Square Press
New York, 1995

The *Shakespeare Set Free* series is an invaluable resource with lesson plans, activites, handouts, and excellent suggestions for rehearsing and performing Shakespeare plays in a classroom setting.

ShakesFear and How to Cure It!
Ralph Alan Cohen
Prestwick House, Inc.
Delaware, 2006

The Friendly Shakespeare: A Thoroughly Painless Guide to the Best of the Bard
Norrie Epstein
Penguin Books
New York, 1994

Brush Up Your Shakespeare!
Michael Macrone
Cader Books
New York, 1990

Shakespeare's Insults: Educating Your Wit
Wayne F. Hill and Cynthia J. Ottchen
Three Rivers Press
New York, 1991

Practical Approaches to Teaching Shakespeare
Peter Reynolds
Oxford University Press
New York, 1991

Scenes From Shakespeare:
A Workbook for Actors
Robin J. Holt
McFarland and Co.
London, 1988

101 Theatre Games for Drama
Teachers, Classroom Teachers
& Directors
Mila Johansen
Players Press Inc.
California, 1994

THEATER AND PERFORMANCE

Impro: Improvisation and the Theatre
Keith Johnstone
Routledge Books
London, 1982

A Dictionary of Theatre Anthropology:
The Secret Art of the Performer
Eugenio Barba and Nicola Savarese
Routledge
London, 1991

THEATER GAMES

Theatre Games for Young Performers
Maria C. Novelly
Meriwether Publishing
Colorado, 1990

Improvisation for the Theater
Viola Spolin
Northwestern University Press
Illinois, 1983

Theater Games for Rehearsal:
A Director's Handbook
Viola Spolin
Northwestern University Press
Illinois, 1985

PLAY DIRECTING

Theater and the Adolescent Actor:
Building a Successful School Program
Camille L. Poisson
Archon Books
Connecticut, 1994

Directing for the Theatre
W. David Sievers
Wm. C. Brown, Co.
Iowa, 1965

The Director's Vision: Play Direction
from Analysis to Production
Louis E. Catron
Mayfield Publishing Co.
California, 1989

INTERNET RESOURCES

http://www.folger.edu
The Folger Shakespeare Library's web
site has lesson plans, primary sources,
study guides, images, workshops,
programs for teachers and students,
and much more. The definitive
Shakespeare website for educators,
historians and all lovers of the Bard.

http://www.shakespeare.mit.edu.
The Complete Works of
William Shakespeare.
All complete scripts for *The
30-Minute Shakespeare* series were
originally downloaded from this site
before editing. Links to other internet
resources.

http://www.LoMonico.com/
Shakespeare-and-Media.htm
http://shakespeare-and-media
.wikispaces.com
Michael LoMonico is Senior
Consultant on National Education
for the Folger Shakespeare Library.
His *Seminar Shakespeare 2.0* offers a
wealth of information on how to use
exciting new approaches and online
resources for teaching Shakespeare.

http://www.freesound.org.
A collaborative database of sounds
and sound effects.

http://www.wordle.net.
A program for creating "word clouds"
from the text that you provide. The
clouds give greater prominence to
words that appear more frequently in
the source text.

http://www.opensourceshakespeare
.org.
This site has good searching capacity.

http://shakespeare.palomar.edu/
default.htm
Excellent links and searches

http://shakespeare.com/
Write like Shakespeare,
Poetry Machine, tag cloud

http://www.shakespeare-online.com/

http://www.bardweb.net/

http://www.rhymezone.com/
shakespeare/
Good searchable word and phrase
finder.
Or by lines:
http://www.rhymezone.com/
shakespeare/toplines/

http://shakespeare.mcgill.ca/
Shakespeare and Performance
research team

http://www.enotes.com/william-
shakespeare

Needless to say, the internet goes on and on with valuable Shakespeare resources.
The ones listed here are excellent starting points and will set you on your way in the
great adventure that is Shakespeare.

NICK NEWLIN has performed a comedy and variety act for international audiences for twenty-seven years. Since 1996, he has conducted an annual play directing residency affiliated with the Folger Shakespeare Library in Washington, D.C. Newlin received a BA with Honors from Harvard University in 1982 and an MA in Theater with an emphasis in Play Directing from the University of Maryland in 1996.

THE 30-MINUTE SHAKESPEARE

A MIDSUMMER NIGHT'S DREAM
978-1-935550-00-6

ROMEO AND JULIET
978-1-935550-01-3

MUCH ADO ABOUT NOTHING
978-1-935550-03-7

MACBETH
978-1-935550-02-0

THE MERRY WIVES OF WINDSOR
978-1-935550-05-1

TWELFTH NIGHT
978-1-935550-04-4

AVAILABLE IN FALL 2010

AS YOU LIKE IT
978-1-935550-06-8

LOVE'S LABOR'S LOST
978-1-935550-07-5

THE COMEDY OF ERRORS
978-1-935550-08-2

KING LEAR
978-1-935550-09-9

HENRY IV, PART 1
978-1-935550-11-2

OTHELLO
978-1-935550-10-5

All plays $7.95, available in bookstores everywhere

"Nick Newlin's 30-minute play cuttings are perfect for students who have no experience with Shakespeare. Each 30-minute mini-play is a play in itself with a beginning, middle, and end." —Michael Ellis-Tolaydo, Department of Theater, Film, and Media Studies, St Mary's College of Maryland

PHOTOCOPYING AND PERFORMANCE RIGHTS

WITHDRAWN FOR DISCARD

CPSIA information can be obtained at www.ICGtesting.com
Printed in the USA
LVOW06s2036281115

464373LV00001B/1/P